The Learning-Driven Organisation Model; An Ecosystem for Organisational Learning

Authors

Alaa Garad & Jeff Gold

© 2018 Garad and Gold

Table of Contents

Introduction iii

The desired outcomes of this model 1
    Organisational Learning 3
Organisational Learning Culture 7
Flow of Learning 11
    Towards a Learning-Driven Organisation 12
Organizational Learning leads to performance improvement 14
Aim of the LDO Model 16
Research Methodology 17
Data Gathering and Analysis 18
Examples of OL Mechanisms based on empirical evidence 21
    Findings 21
    Discussion 25
Dynamics of the relationship between OL Culture and OL Mechanisms
.... 29
Conclusion 35
The way forward 37
References 38

About the Authors 45

Introduction

The authors present a model of the Learning-Driven Organisation (LDO); a model that considers the whole ecosystem, its subsystems and considers the importance of technology, digitalization and dataism. The LDO Model answers three key questions:

1. What makes an organisation learning-driven?
2. How and why the learning ecosystem works organisation-wide?
3. How can we measure organisational learning?

They authors begin with a consideration of some of the key ideas relating to organisational learning, learning culture and measurement of the results of learning. They then consider the development of an empirically-based model of the learning-driven organisation. Ecosystem is defined by Oxford Dictionary (2018) as *a biological community of interacting organisms and their physical environment.* This is how organisations are behaving nowadays; we argue that organisations are ecosystems that have its own interacting dynamics on the one hand and on the other hand, they interact with their physical and virtual or digital environment. Learning is crucial to facilitate this ecosystem and helps it to sustain and grow at the organisational level. The literature on organisational learning has emphasised its importance as critical for every organisation[1]; moreover, there is a consensus that learning could be an organisation's only source of sustainability[2]. There are a range of pressures on why leaders and managers need to become learning-driven. This includes how much attention needs to be given to collaboration as well as to competition or whether adding benefit to communities and society in general needs to be given more prominence. This calls into question the extent to which the provision of learning will and should

---

[1] (e.g. Argyris and Schon, 1978; Argyris, 1996; Fioretti, 2007; Garratt, 2000
[2] Argote, 2013; Lipshitz *et al.*, 2007; Marsick and Watkins, 2003

extend beyond organisational boundaries and bring some results to society at large. As has been exemplified by recent problems such as toxic exhaust fumes or other misdirected waste, value needs to be given to impact of learning beyond organisational boundaries. It also has to include how technology in all its forms has the potential transform our lives but also the possibility to destroy. This might include technology that is used to exploit and denigrate human effort and reward and even replace humans or whether it helps to explore potential, creativity and development[3]. In the same vein there has been very little research done on the overall "big" picture of the effects of the effect of *digitalisation* on organisations though the digitalization of society and business is marching forward at an increasing speed, calling for more research on the phenomenon[4].

The authors of this model, argue that learning was, has become and always will be a critical process. At a time when so many organisations, the people in those organisations and those who depend on organisations to live their lives, are faced with many and often contradictory pressures, learning - by conscious human beings - needs to be pursued strategically, critically and embedded in how we live and work. The model begin with a brief overview of literature relating to organisational learning before considering the key elements of what the authors call a Learning-Driven Organisation (LDO). They then report emerging results of the development of the LDO in an effort to create meaning structures for organisational learning.

---

[3] Mitic *et al*, 2017; Roztocki & Weistroffer, 2015; Gilianinia *et al*, 2013
[4] Kuusisto, (2017)

The desired outcomes of this model

The LDO model caters for several stakeholders; if effectively implemented, the following outcomes are expected to be achieved:

Stakeholder	Outcomes

Organisations	1) **Increase**
	   a. Productivity
	   b. Market share
	   c. Development of new products and services
	   d. Profitability
	   e. Employee engagement and satisfaction
	   f. Wellbeing
	   g. Resilience
	2) **Reduces:**
	   a. Workplace accidents
	   b. Absenteeism
	   c. Turnover
	   d. Waste
	   e. Consumption

Executives	1) Provides a clear roadmap towards achieving organisation's ambition 2) Improves dialogue with all stakeholders 3) Reduces negative energy 4) Better optimization of the most valuable resource i.e. 'time'
Shareholders/Trustees	1) Increases Profitability/surplus 2) Ensures sustainability, business continuity 3) Helps the organisation to become a 'good citizen'
Employees	1) Better well-being

	2) More recognition and appreciation from management 3) Enhanced job security 4) Clear career path 5) Less negative energy 6) Blame-free workplace 7) Pride and engagement
Customers	1) Continuously improved produced and services 2) Two-way communication with the organisation 3) Recognition for the feedback and even for complaints. 4) Ethically responsible practice. 5) Opportunities for co-creation of new products/services.
Partners/Suppliers	1) Opportunities for learning and exchange of knowledge 2) Replacing the tension and win-lose approach with win-win approach 3) Better business terms and conditions 4) Enhanced transparency and integrity 5) Payment on time 6) Honouring commitments.
Society	1) God citizen which do not harm the flora, environment etc. 2) Ethical business practice 3) Creating more jobs and opportunities
Regulators	1) Transparency 2) Compliance 3) Continuous improvement
Research Community	1) Access to data 2) Connecting the dots and demystifying various phenomenon 3) Continuous learning about learning

Organisational Learning

Organizational learning (OL) has been and remains a source of interest among researchers and practitioners, but it is also a point of widespread controversy and confusion on learning in or by organizations[5]. No one single perspective in current learning theory is sufficient to capture fully the multiple connections and possibilities that learning creates and from which it emerges[6]. Nevertheless, it is claimed that OL has been a critical process ensuring the very existence of whole industries and without OL, entirely new products and industries would not have been spawned[7]. Some authors[8] have been more skeptical about claims for OL, view the concept as an 'oxymoron' where learning can occur but can also be undermined by processes of organising. Learning and organising can result in tensions which limit the potential of learning. Other authors highlight a range of barriers to OL, such as fear, stress and lack of motivation at a personal level, strict work rules, narrow jobs, and blame cultures within an organisation[9]. Others are more positive about the potential of OL. Dixon, (1999, p. 6), for example, defined OL as *'the intentional use of learning processes at the individual, group and system level to continuously transform the organisation in a direction that is increasingly satisfying to its stakeholders'*. Dixon's definition focuses on the view that learning should lead to the satisfaction of an organisation's stakeholders; it depends on the use of processes without much focus on the culture. Garratt (2000) suggested a three-level model (depicted in Table 1 and Fig 1) that identifies three levels of learning, where the first level *policy learning* represent the external effectiveness, the *operational learning* represents the internal efficiency while the *strategic learning* represents the integration of these two other levels which seems comprehensive model as it tackles the various aspects and stakeholders within and beyond the organisation's boundaries.

---

[5] Jyothibabu, *et al.*, 2010
[6] Antonacopoulou, 2006
[7] DiBella and Nevis, 1998
[8] Weick and Westley (1996)
[9] Schilling and Kluger (2009)

Table 1- Summary of Garratt's Levels of Learning

Learning Level	Description
Policy Learning	Policy learning is about managers, directors and staff combining to make sense of the patterns in the turbulent and fast-changing external environment. It means systematic awareness of and reflection, action and feedback on changes in the political, physical, economic, social, and technological and trade environments. It is part of *total organisational learning* and cannot be handled in isolation.
Strategic Learning	Strategic learning is about monitoring the changing external world, reviewing the organisation's position in these changes, making risk assessments to protect and develop enterprise, broadly deploying its scarce resources to achieve its purpose and ensuring that there are feedback procedures to measure the effectiveness of any strategy being implemented. Strategic learning must be set in the context of agreed policies.
Operational Learning	Operational learning is day-to-day learning by managers and staff which does not require over-analysis leading to 'analysis-paralysis'.

Source: Adapted from Garratt (2000, pp. 3-11)

Fig 1 - Three levels of learning

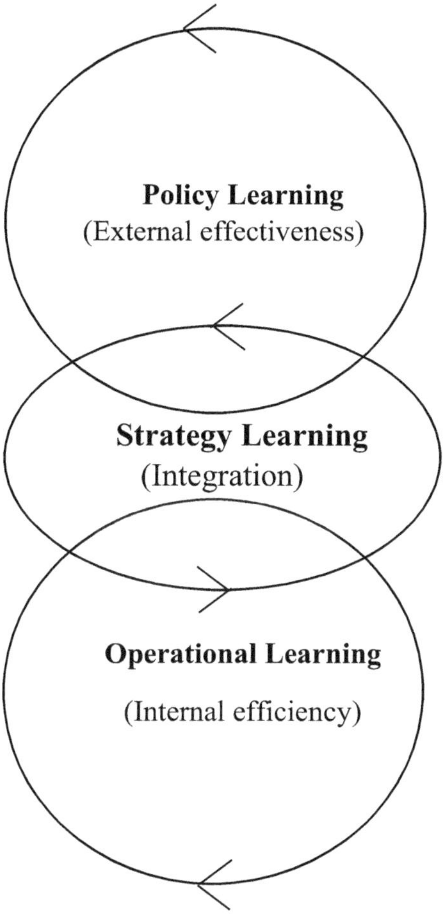

Policy Learning
(External effectiveness)

Strategy Learning
(Integration)

Operational Learning
(Internal efficiency)

Source: Garratt, (2000, p. 5)

Dixon and Garratt both imply a degree of intention that stimulates an OL process. Acquiring information to make knowledge that forms intelligence that allows changing behaviour by humans and increasingly, non-humans. For humans, this can involve reflection to reveal values and assumptions, insights into practice allowing a revision of attitudes, deciding responsibly and wisely. Some authors concluded that an organisation's employees can create, acquire and transfer knowledge that allows the organization to adapt to unpredictable market conditions more quickly than competitors and by the acquisition and dissemination of knowledge, an organization can shape its future[10]. These may, or may not, lead to improvement in performance[11]. Frequently considered as tacit knowledge, it is quite possible that learning can remain hidden or unrecognized, deliberately or otherwise. For example, Crossan et al[12]. model of OL casts 'intuiting' as an initial process of seeing patterns which become possible ideas for application through explanation and sharing through 'interpreting'. However, such processes might not flow unhindered. Models of OL emphasize the need for a consideration of contextual features and space to enable knowledge sharing and conversion[13]. Values play a crucial role where learning occurs on the basis of meanings made in local contexts, often beyond the sight of leaders and managers[14].

---

[10] Senge (1990) and Fibuch & Roberston (2017)
[11] Brockbank *et al.*, 2002
[12] Crossan et al's (1999)
[13] Nonaka et al. 2000
[14] Fenwick 2008

Organisational Learning Culture

What makes learning distinctly organisational? A question that has been asked by many authors where some of them argued that OL is an 'oxymoron' and learning does not exist in parallel with organising[15]; they have been sceptical about the body of knowledge of OL as they think there appear to be more reviews of OL than the substance to review. They suggest addressing OL from a culture perspective.

Culture could be defined as "set of values, beliefs, and feelings, together with artefacts that are created, inherited, shared and transmitted within one group of people and that's, in part distinguish that group from others"[16]. Others defined organisational culture as the relatively stable ways of perceiving the world and the action strategies that an organisation has learned from experience[17]; therefore if the culture is rigid and strong enough to resist change then it will become a dysfunctional, however, if the culture is learning oriented, adaptive and flexible[18] then an organisation can have perpetual learning. This may implies that, as the culture changes, it may not be uniformly distributed throughout the organisation; hence a mechanism could be developed to establish and maintain the uniformity Organisational learning culture (OLC) is the culture that fosters the practices of acquisition of information, distribution and transfer of learning and recognition for learning-based application[19].

Culture and structures are two main conditions for organisational learning. If structures represent the relatively tangible 'hardware' of organisational learning, the organisational culture represent the

---

[15] Weik and Westley (1996, p. 440)
[16] Cook and Yanow (1993, p. 379).
[17] Schein (1990, 2004)
[18] Senge, 2006
[19] Yang et al. 2004 cited in Banerjee et al. 2017

'software'[20]. In the same vein, Garvin[21] described the organisation that embraces and foster culture of learning as a learning organisation 'an organisation skilled at creating, acquiring, and transferring knowledge, and at modifying its behaviour to reflect new knowledge and insights'. Organisational learning culture (OLC) not only has a significant impact on creating organisational knowledge and on the overall organisation's performance but also organisational learning culture can be a vital aspect of organisational culture and the core of a learning organisation"[22]. A successful organisation is an organisation that considers learning as a success factor in business and is able to learn and integrate learning in its functions[23]. Fostering a learning culture will not only help employees to show high levels of performance but also will help to retain those employees in the organisation[24]. Organisations that foster learning culture attract knowledgeable employees, enhance their level of commitment toward the organisation[25] and reduce the employees' intention to leave the organisation[26]. A culture oriented towards learning is essential for promoting learning in organisations in a productive and sustainable way[27]. Considering the plethora of literature on learning culture and its role in transforming organisations, the authors of this model believe that OLC, is the base of the learning-driven organisation pyramid.

Leaders and managers can become learning-driven but learning needs to be critical of assumptions made, the values that inform those assumptions and the consequences for what is done in practice. Because of this, it is essential to investigate learning processes within and beyond the traditional boundaries of organisation and how such processes can contribute towards 'organisational learning'. The concept of OL is not

---

[20] Friedman et al. 2001, p. 760
[21] Garvin (1993, p. 80)
[22] Wang et al., 2007, p. 156; Robelo and Gomes 2010
[23] Maquardt, 2002; Shafei et al., 2011
[24] Malik et al. (2011)
[25] Jo and Joo, 2011
[26] Islam et al., 2015: Perryer et al., 2010; Wong et al., 2012
[27] Robelo and Gomes, 2010

new, and has been present in the management literature for many years but it became widely recognised only in the 1990s[28].

Dixon (*1999*) argues that, in order for OL to occur, private meaning structures should be made more accessible and moved to the accessible meaning structures. Moreover, the latter should be pushed towards collective meaning structures. This is further explained in the table below (Table 2):

Table 2- Types of Meaning Structures

Meaning Structures	What does it mean
Private Meaning	Accumulated learning experiences and knowledge about the organisation and the individual's own processes. Individuals do not tend to share their private meaning structures for various reasons. However, the more individuals are willing to make it available to others in the organisation, the more the organisation is able to learn.
Accessible Meaning	These are the meaning structures that individuals are willing to share with others in the organisation. It is analogous to the hallways of the organisation where exchanges take place and where ideas get tested against the thinking of others. When these meaning structures are made accessible to others then the data on which it is based can be challenged. Hallways are places where 'collective meaning' is made and constructed.
Collective Meaning	This is the collective meaning which organisational members hold in common. It can be represented in the norms, strategies and assumptions which specify how work gets done. It may be codified in policies and procedures. Collective meaning is like having a

---

[28] Popova-Nowak and Cseh, 2015; Argote, 2011

| | *storeroom* where the mementos of the past are kept. It is the history of the organisation and it is the *glue* that holds organisational members together. It provides a sense of belonging and community and it saves the organisation's time. However, it can also have a negative impact on the organisation when it became obsolete or inhibits learning. |

Source: Adapted from Dixon (1999, p.45-49)

Despite the importance of the topic, there seems to be a lack of consensus regarding the relevant definitions and the methods of practicing learning so that it becomes organisational.

Flow of Learning

As the links between individual learning and organisation-wide learning is instrumental for OL to occur, it is necessary to understand the dynamics of such a relationship. There are some instances where individual members of an organisation do not act, think or reflect on behalf of their organisation where the organisational environment does not provide *Learning Meadows*[29]. Therefore, when learning occurs and knowledge has been acquired, it stays in the individuals minds rather than being diffused into the organisation's fabric where individuals become mere *'carriers of learning'*[30]; in this case the knowledge leaves when these carriers leave the organisation. Building on this idea, organisational members in relation to their learning can be described as:

1. Learning Connectors:
- active members, learning agents who think, inquire, reflect and act on behalf of the organisation;

2. Learning Incubators:
- members who acquire knowledge however, they are not able to bring to the organisation due to absence of system or complacency;

3. Learning Insulators:
- members who are disengaged and do not participate in learning activities.

---

[29] Wilhelm (2005)
[30] Argyris and Schon (1996)

In order for OL to occur, organisations need to encourage their members to act as learning connectors, and should put measures in place and facilitate *learning meadows* that bring learning incubators on board and finally identify the learning insulators and put them on track by inquiring into the root cause of behind their attitudes and behaviours. Failing to provide for the possibility of transforming individual learning into "organizational" learning is a missed opportunity and could pose a risk to sustainability or progress.

Towards a Learning-Driven Organisation

Visionaries and advocates of OL provided little guidance on how to put organisational learning into practice in order to 'get there from here'[31]. A necessary condition for systematically promoting OL is the existence of OL structures in which the learning process can be carried out; the need to test organisational learning mechanisms can guide managerial actions towards reinforcing and fostering creativity[32]. Popper and Lipshitz's (1998, 2000) work is considered to be the first attempt to give clarity to the nature of organisational learning mechanisms (OLMs) as they provided the first comprehensive definition of these, defined as *institutionalized arrangements that allow organizations to systematically collect, analyze, store, retrieve and use information that is relevant to the performance of the organisation and its members*[33]

Other authors[34] developed a theoretical framework of OLMs that classified three broad categories, namely cognitive, structural and procedural mechanisms as follows:

---

[31] Friedman et *al* (2001)
[32] Mitki *et al* (2008)
[33] Cirella *et al* .2017
[34] Shani and Docherty (2003, 2008)

a) Cognitive Mechanisms:
• Clarity of strategy, connection strategy-activities, coherence strategy-training, learning encouragement culture, and sharing of common language.
b) Structural Mechanisms:
• Information between colleagues, knowledge of who does what, participation in teamwork, continuous improvement, and reference for having support.
c) Procedural Mechanisms:
• Knowledge of resources and objectives, knowledge of controlling criteria, midway reviews, post-project reviews and routines about use of archives.

The authors of this model believe that there is a dire need for clarity and further classification of OLMs as this can help organizations to construct meanings of their learning practices and therefore will enable the conversion of learning into strategies, policies and procedures i.e. to make OL more 'actionable'.

Organizational Learning leads to performance improvement

In spite of the confusion on the meaning of OL there is almost a consensus on its importance to the organizations' performance in the long-term as well as the short-term. Authors such as Senge, 1990; and many other authors[35] argued that learning is an important way to improve performance in the long-term, and in the near future, organisations that can utilize people's abilities, commitment and learning capacity in all the levels can accomplish their goals and realize their vision. Simply, organisations can improve their performances through OL. In order to confirm such claims about OL's importance, researchers have attempted to develop measures to see if and how its impact can indeed be measured objectively or based on judgments or opinions[36]. To measure OL, either we measure OL capabilities or OL processes, in addition, learning effects can be measured on an individual level, a team level and an organisational level[37]. Jyothibabu *et al.* (2010) attempted to develop a conceptual approach for measuring OL by merging the enablers' model[38] and the performance model[39]. That approach incorporated learning enablers, learning results (at individual, group and organizational level) and performance outcomes. However it can be argued that Individual Learning Levels (ILL), Group Learning Levels (GLL) and Organisational Learning Levels (OLL) can be considered as enablers as well as an outcome. Therefore there is a need for a clearer approach for measurement that can focus on 'how to' undertake such measurement.

---

[35] Nonaka and Takeuchi, 1995; Sharma, 2003; Marquardt, 2002; Akhavan and Jafari, 2006; Bowen et al. 2006; Saadat and Saadat, 2016
[36] Chiva *et al.*, 2007
[37] Guta, 2014
[38] Crossan *et al.* (1999)
[39] Bontis *et al.* (2002)

It is very crucial to measure OL in order to assess the extent of it in organisations and how it supports the management of the organisation[40]. There is a suggested approach to measure the impact of OL based on errors and mistakes at work[41], however that approach is focused on only on errors and does not take account of the context of organisational climate. However the proposed model confirmed that OL has an impact on organizations' performance. Most considerations of OL focus on one or two elements without taking a holistic approach. For example, some authors[42] focused on the ethos and philosophy that underpin OL. While others focused on individual and team learning cycles from a practice perspective[43] or on OL mechanisms and the process[44]. Few authors focused on the measurement of OL[45]. Although all of the above areas of focus are crucial for learning to occur and be sustained, learning would not occur due to culture only or structure. If learning does not occur, there will be no need for its measurement. Therefore, the authors of this model emphasize the need for an integrative ecosystem that incorporates three components of OL i.e. culture, mechanisms and outcomes.

---

[40] Templeton *et al.* (2002)
[41] Putz *et al.* (2012)
[42] Senge (1990, 2006) and Argyris (1996), Schein (1990, 2004) and Yang *et al.* (2004)
[43] Dixon (1999)
[44] Lipshitz *et al.* (2007), Marsick and Watkins (2003), Friedman *et al.* (2001) and Argote (2013)
[45] Chiva et al (2007), Guta (2014), Crossan *et al.* (1999) and Bontis *et al.* (2002)

Aim of the LDO Model

This LDO Model is an attempt to provide leaders and practitioners in all circumstances and in any type organisation with an opportunity to become the drivers of learning. Based on a critical literature review and informed by primary and secondary data, we suggest that organisations and those who make the key decisions on how they work, need to grasp a way of thinking and working that considers learning holistically, operationally and consider its impacts beyond the boundaries of the operations. In the context of the LDO model, we define learning as: *"The process of modifying organisational behaviour through the use of different processes, practices, methods and activities in drawing lessons learned from within and outside the organisation for the purpose of systematically improving performance and transforming into a learning-driven organisation".* Our assumptions here are that by learning it remains essentially a feature of human existence. However, we must be aware that this might always be the case; humans and non-humans together might become the unit for consideration and beyond[46].

---

[46] Harari, 2016

Research Methodology

The proposed LDO model builds on empirical data collected from two case study organisations in the hospitality sector in Dubai, the UAE. We relied on both primary and secondary data. The reason for selecting these two organisations was that both had been assessed against their organisational learning and overall performance within a national quality award context using Business Excellence Model i.e. EFQM Excellence Model[47]. This assessment is an independent assessment, external and voluntary that was undertaken by a team of volunteer assessors and organised by the Department of Economic Development in Dubai. Due to confidentiality concerns, the names of the organisations would not be disclosed. Organisation A employs 620 employees and it achieved a high score in learning and excellence (685/1000), while organisation B, employs 1200 employees and achieved 285/1000.

---

[47] Details at http://www.efqm.org/what-we-do/assessment/self-assessment

Data Gathering and Analysis

Before starting data analysis a summary of OL practices that were identified from literature review were tabulated and an abbreviation of each Organisational Learning Mechanism (Practice) was given (as shown in Table 3) in order to simplify and systemize the analysis and tracing the 'how' part of the learning. Data was gathered using qualitative semi-structured interviews with forty-four informants from three levels of management i.e. senior management, middle management and front line employees. In addition to the interviews, ten focus groups were run in both organisations where 37 more employees were interviewed. The data gathering methods were used in order to obtain an in-depth understanding of the relevant facts as well as to verify the validity of the interview responses in addition to observation and participation in meetings and strategic planning activities. This was complemented by direct observations for over twelve months and a comprehensive document/archival review. In addition, the authors were informed by a combined sixty years of hands-on experience as assessors and business and organisational development practitioners. One of the authors have assessed over 450 organisations in the Middle East and the other author have been a professor and consultant in Organisational Learning in the UK, Middle East and several other countries. The interview questions were open-ended and aimed to dive deeply in the OL culture, mechanisms, and methods for measuring the results.

Table 3 – the investigated OL Practices

Organisational Learning Practice (OLP):	Code
1. After-Action Review	AAR
2. Benchmarking	BMR
3. Coaching	COA
4. Feedback Loops	FDL
5. Mentoring	MNT
6. Problem-Solving	PSV
7. Quality Award Application	QAW
8. Reflection	RFL
9. Self-Assessment	SAS
10. Suggestion Schemes	SUG
11. Team Learning	TML
12. Two-Way Communication/Dialogue	COM
13. Mystery Shopping	MYS
14. Audits	ADT
15. Cross-Training	CTR

Microsoft Excel was used to record the hand-written responses. During the data analysis phase colour coding was used to identify the pattern for example yellow was used to highlight the explanation of methods, while green was used to highlight the explanation of collective interpretation of meaning..etc (shown in Table 4). The number of colours and table has below has emerged during the analysis of data as it was analyzed without use of any other software but MS Excel.

Table 4 – Responses' Colour Codes

Colour	Used to designate
Yellow	Method – i.e. how OL practice is being implemented, its scope of implementation, and generation of information.
Blue	How information and learning lessons are integrated into organisational context.
Green	Collective interpretation and communication of learning
Orange	Perceived improvement/action taken based on interpreted meaning
Pink	Any practice that is not being reviewed in the literature and general understanding of OLPs

Examples of OL Mechanisms based on empirical evidence

Findings

Based on the critical review of literature, we identified the fifteen mechanism for organisational learning and when investigated within the two case organisations, we were able to classify them into three categories i.e. organisation-wide learning, team learning and individual learning, (as shown in Figure 1).

Figure 1 – classification of OL Mechanisms against the three levels of Organizational Learning

There are at least fifteen mechanisms to facilitate application of OL in the two case organisations, for example, After Action Reviews, Mystery Shopping, Self-Assessment,… etc. are regularly undertaken and the outcomes are documented and incorporated into the organizations' policies and procedures. The meetings for AAR itself are being considered as a means for collective interpretation of information since the members of the committees are representatives of all departments across the organisation. Responses from all interviewees were clear and confirms their understanding of the organisation's approach and philosophy about learning. As an example of learning from others' experience formally and informally, the two case organisations are consciously proactive in acquiring knowledge, reflecting on it and generating their own model that is distributed and communicated to all business units then it becomes a components of its performance management system; When it was realised that the benchmarking practices are not streamlined and it was felt that they can be better utilized and employed in a more structured manner, the management developed guidelines for benchmarking and included them into the organisation management system i.e. they have a documented policy accompanied by an explanation of the process with relevant literature on the practice. The Learning and Development Department in both organisations plays a major role in fostering OL; coaching and mentoring were found to be key methods for facilitating OL practices on individual as well as organisational level.

Information is shared with everyone, even if it is not directly related to their job role and job rotation practice is believed to help in this regard. There is a continuous and open dialogue among the employees, vertically and horizontally, which has been witnessed and confirmed by all interviewees. Intranet is extensively utilized in new information dissemination and lesson learned. Both organisations summarize lessons learnt, incidents and new issues in a weekly newsletter that is distributed to every employee by email and posted on the Intranet.

Managers are empowered to identify and send their subordinates to relevant training programmes. Actions and delegation are provided within the empowerment matrix. As issues and learnt lessons are documented, they become subject to internal and external audit and follow up. There is a variety of channels that help both case study organisations to obtain feedback on the spot directly from the guests, saving the guests' time and giving them an opportunity to explain in more details and receive acknowledgement of the issues, and, sometimes, a solution. It was noticed that some minor feedback is obtained immediately and is not disseminated or documented such as single feedback about a meal, however in case of the same feedback occurrence, then an investigation takes place and the issues get documented and more appropriate actions are taken. It was also noticed that employees are being dealt with as internal customers; this concept is widely spread among management and supervisory levels. The feedback obtained is subject to a complete loop where it is disseminated through emails, Intranet and meetings. As mentioned above, the direct involvement of senior management in most of the practices including Feedback Handling helps the organisation to implement smoothly the proposed actions based on the generated information.

It was found that the organisations investigated in this research enjoy encouraging a learning environment at all levels with a lesser degree in Case B. According to the Argyris and Schon[48], there is a type of learning that results in individuals acting in a way that inhibits Productive OL. For example individuals may learn to create and maintain taboos that keep critical issues un-discussable, or use scapegoating, or camouflage intentions and systematic patterns of deception. Review of the 44 interviewees' views showed that such practices did not exist in any of the two case studies. Employees (colleagues) at both case organisations are undertaking series of continuous inquiry on behalf of their organisation; in this endeavor, they are acting as learning agents of their organisations, hence it is believed that Organisational Learning is occurring and is sustained at both organisations but with different level of maturity. This is supported in the literature where inquiry does not become organisational unless undertaken by individuals who function as agents of an organisation to which they belong[49]. Throughout the data collection stage, interviewees were speaking the same language; it was evident that the case organisations have managed to make most of the *private meanings accessible meaning,* moreover, the *accessible meaning*

---

[48] According to the Argyris and Schon (1996)
[49] Argyris and Schon (1996, p.11)

has become *collective meaning* that was stored, not only inside the individuals minds, but also on many forms of storage such as the intranet, websites, public folder, policies and procedures and many more mediums in the form of manuals and handbooks. Furthermore, that collective meaning is being shared with other entities (i.e. other sister organisations). '*Collective meaning is that meaning which all members hold in common*'[50]

Discussion

Why a LDO Model?

As we aim to propose an ecosystem OL model, we tried to understand and showcase how learning can become organisational as well as strategic, and how change can be facilitated and lead from lessons learned. In doing so, we critically reviewed enormous number of artifacts and documented OL and LO models. Nevertheless the documented organisational learning models and frameworks arguing that those models are often formulated at a high level of generalization that is difficult to translate into action; 'organisational actors require relatively clear milestones that can guide the process of trying to foster organisational learning'[51]. This LDO Model is an outcome of sixteen years' study to create meaning structures for organisational learning. Every day, people in organizations face problems of various degrees of complication at all levels. While some problems can be easily solved, others defy quick solution and can produce and reproduce conflicting interpretations of what is happening. Such problems require a great deal of listening, understanding, reflection and analysis to understand the nature and complexity then find a way of moving forward. This necessitates therefore:

---

[50] Dixon (1999)

[51] Friedman *et al.* (2001, p. 758)

a) the interpretations of the different people involved (including yourself)
b) the different goals and expectations of those involved
c) a need to construct a way of proceeding

In many cases, the way issues are framed, locks people into a way of thinking and behaving which might fix things in the short term but eventually brings back the original conditions of concern. In current times, we need learning to cope with exponential data and information overflow, and the new concepts and technologies which are evolving every day. We have already seen development such as the gig economy, expert economy, Internet of Things (IoT), Industries 4.0, smart cities, Decision Support Systems (DSS), smart products, drones, and digital medicine and so on, with more to come. It soon becomes clear that existing standards and frameworks cannot cope with the challenges; the major missing element throughout most of existing frameworks and models is 'learning'. Learning should be the core element of any standard, moreover, there is a major need for a model that develops an ecosystem that helps organizations shape their future. Until now, learning has mostly been 'caged' into literature and theory; even those leaders who claim to support learning do not always know where to start or how to sustain what they have started. Learning can be structured into a sustainable system that consists of a repository of good practices that can act as an-eye opener rather a descriptive 'cookbook'.

The proposed LDO Model paints a picture of what learning may really look like, making the intangible tangible through interpreting the theoretical frameworks and diverse learning thesis into a language that people understand, digest and develop enthusiasm for to act and transform knowledge into actions to feed and sustain an ecosystem for learning.

As our society seems to enter rapidly into a new era of techno-humanism and dataism, it is obvious that there will be a pivotal need for a fast-learning approach to extract the lessons and package the takeaways for busy human beings and non-human beings who may exist sooner or later. Unless mankind learns fast, and set its direction, then sooner than later the humankind will lose its humanity and intelligence will prevails over consciousness (Harari 2016)

The LDO mode resonates with the World Bank Group approach towards Learning.

> "Learning is key to solving development challenges, and to meeting the World Bank Group's twin goals of ending poverty and building shared prosperity. Development progress is often challenged by multiple interdependent factors; mitigating these factors requires change that can be harnessed through continuous learning". (WBG, 2017)

ISO 10018:2012 (ISO, 2017) highlighted the importance of leaning, and established that learning processes may apply to a person or collectively to an organisation. An organization should recognize that people learn in different ways. The LDO model is instrumental in integrating theory with practice and establishing an ecosystem that connects the dots and proposes an integrated model for organisational learning as a vehicle for the Learning-Driven Organisation.

The LDO Model:

As an outcome of empirical research, the authors have proposed a model that does not 'straightjacket' the practice of learning neither it is meant to be a prescriptive model; it is meant to be an open source of guidelines and building blocks of what works at the time of publishing. It is meant to be alive model that takes into consideration the dynamics of business, political, social and technological environment. The LDO Ecosystem model consists of three subsystems namely, culture, mechanisms and results, as illustrated in Figure 2.

Figure 2 – Three subsystems that form the organisational learning ecosystem

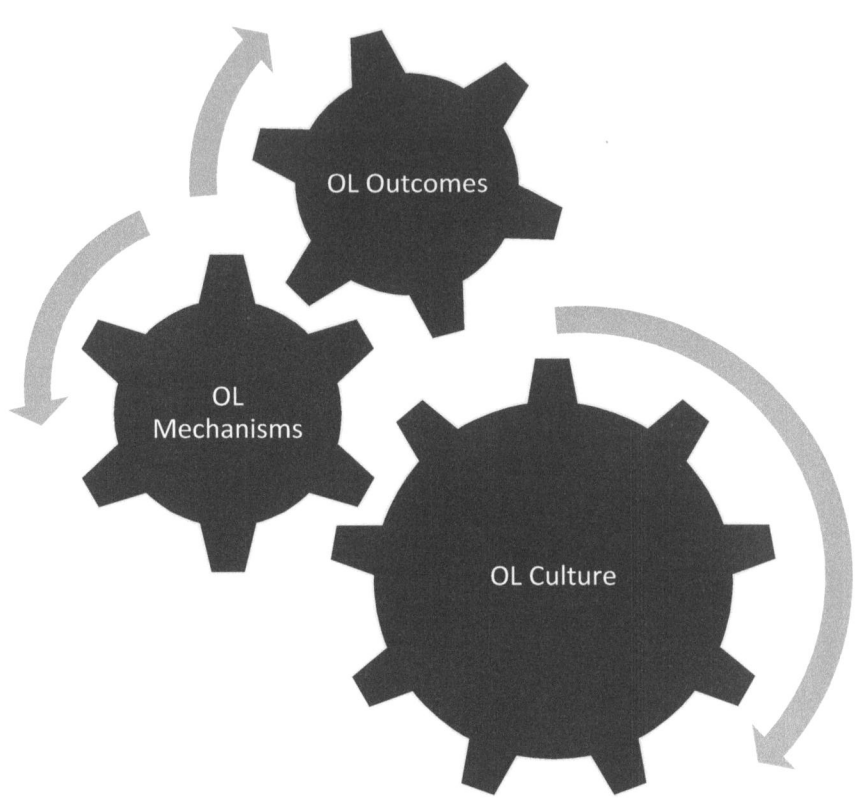

Dynamics of the relationship between OL Culture and OL Mechanisms

We assume that OL Culture and OL Mechanisms are so embedded and intertwined to the extent that it is sometimes challenging to separate or label them; culture and mechanisms go together hand in hand. We struggled to visualize such a relationship between those two sub-systems in the global OL Ecosystem of the organisation, therefore we have used a Ship's wheel to visualize these two parts of the LDO sub-systems i.e. OL Culture and OL Mechanisms. As shown in Figure 3, OL Culture acts as the handles of the ship's wheel that helps in smoothing the directions and keeps the ship (the organisation) on track. The LDO Model assumes that OL Mechanisms are spread over three levels i.e. Individual Learning, Team Learning and Organisation-wide Learning. IL is assumed to occur within the workplace or and/or outside as it is an ongoing cognitive and behavioral state; IL is perceived as the core of organisational learning, where the organisation's members engage in learning (as learning agents). However, it does not operate in isolation from the other two levels of learning. It is represented by the inner core of the Ship's Wheel. The following figure illustrates the dynamic correlation between the Organisational Learning Culture (OLC) and the three levels of learning.

Figure 3 – The relationship between OL Culture and OL Mechanisms

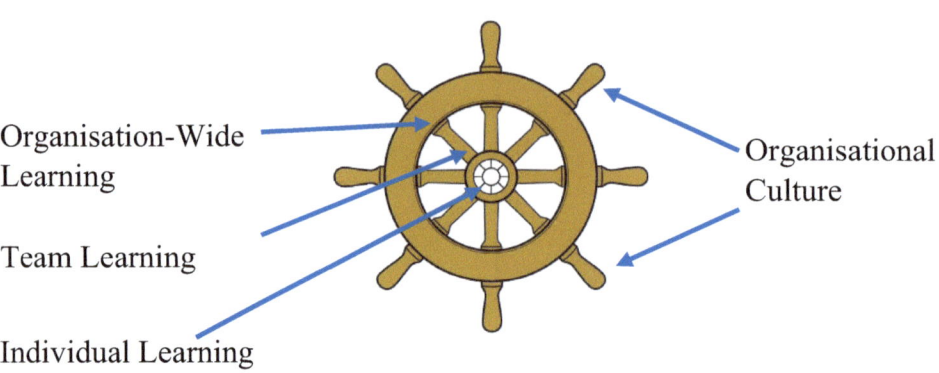

The three subsystems namely a) Organisational Learning Culture – OLC: why we do what we do – this represents the first sub-system in the LDO. b) Organisational Learning Mechanisms - OLM: How we do what we do; which represents the second sub-system in the LDO and c) Organisational Learning Outcomes - OLO: what we get as a result of what we do; this represents the third sub-system in the LDO as shown in Figure 4.

Figure 4 – The LDO Ecosystem Rationale

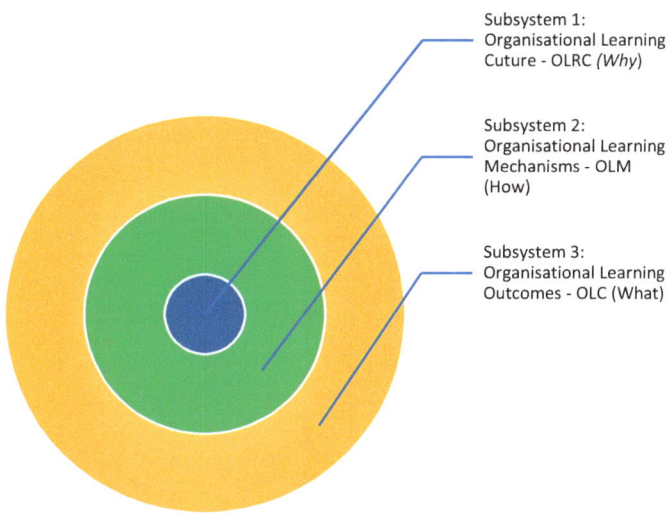

Developed by the authors, inspired by Sinek (2009)

S1: Organisational Learning Culture (Why)

Inspired by Wittgenstein, we use a river in flow. At one level, organisation culture acts like the nutrients that enable a river's life. It is the history from past formation that sets what is allowed and what is not allowed. It can enrich and nurture learning and all other favoured approaches but it can also can prevent. The bed of the river interacts with its boundaries, or the two banks that shape the river. The shaping can be understood as structures and systems, more or less permanent in a culture but subject to possible disturbance, collapses and redirections. Then there is the flow of the river, everyday life (unless it dries up!) that is affected by the structures and systems but can also be the instigators of change to those structures and systems. Much of the life is visible and can appear normal or under pressure but much can be hidden below the surface. This can make life difficult to understand if you are not in the flow or observing a static flow from the banks. Without understanding organisation culture, it becomes difficult to gain acceptance of change and to reap the benefit of what can be learned. Culture may be assessed and addressed though not limited to the following dimensions of practice for learning:

> 1.1 Leaders establish and nurture learning culture organization-wide.
> 1.2 Leaders are role models for learning.
> 1.3 Trust is evident organisation-wide
> 1.4 Transparency and openness for learning.
> 1.5 Continuous improvement is embedded.
> 1.6 People are engaged at all levels.
> 1.7 Teamwork is encouraged and rewarded organisation-wide.
> 1.8 Autonomy and empowerment in the decision making process.

S2: Organisational Learning Mechanisms (How):

Organisational learning structure is defined; (Friedman *et* al. 2001) various learning processes, procedures, and activities are actively employed organisation-wide. This may include -but not limited to-, reflection, coaching, mentoring, after-action review, suggestions schemes and benchmarking:

S2.1 – OLM - Policy Level

> 2.1 There are various channels where the organisation can listen to its customers, partners and other stakeholders.
> 2.2 Feedback from all stakeholders is considered and acted upon
> 2.3 Learning from others is encouraged, and supported organisation-wide
> 2.4 The organisation participates in knowledge acquisition and dissemination activities outside the organisation, nationally and internationally

S2.2 – OLM - Strategic Level

2.5 Organisation strategy sets a direction for learning and responds to the consequences
2.6 Budget for organisational learning is secured and responsibility allocated
2.7 Learning is articulated, shared, understood and implemented.
2.8 Learning needs are identified, acted upon and outcome is measured for individuals, teams, and organisation wide
2.9 Ongoing processes exist to consider critically the meaning of learning.
2.10 Learning outcomes are publicly acknowledged and published on a regular basis
2.11 Suggestions can flow into and within the organisation e.g. idea management systems, and internal blogs.

S2.3 – OLM - Operational Level

2.12 There are various types of activities to help people understand how they learn.
2.13 The organisation is engaged in learning activities that extends their previous boundaries.
2.14 Individuals and team are recognised for learning.
2.15 Appropriate mechanisms such as coaching and mentoring are employed to engage and involve at all organisational levels.
2.16 Lessons learnt are documented, classified, communicated and utilised organisation wide.
2.17 People at all levels have fair access to information appropriate to their needs.
2.18 People have fair access to support at all levels.
2.19 People are encouraged and supported to acquire further academic education and qualifications where applicable.

2.20 Appropriate technology is employed to support and facilitate learning.

S3: Organisational Learning Outcomes (What):

Measurement enables the assessment of achievement. Measurement is crucial to know the extent to which the targeted results have been accomplished; not only this, but also assessing the appropriateness of the employed learning mechanisms and approaches.

3.1. Learning is measured throughout the organisation.
3.2. People are aware how learning benefits them at their individual role and at the organisation level.
3.3. Strategic and operational decisions are informed by learning outcomes and organization's leaders are able to give specific examples of strategic adaption.
3.4. Learning helps the organisation to achieve its strategic objectives.
3.5. Employed learning mechanisms are reviewed so that the organisation is fully aware of what works and what does not.
3.6. Learning enables the organisation to innovate and develop, or improve, products and services.
3.7. Learning enables the organisation to predict and shape its future.

Conclusion

The LDO Model has built on the extensive contributions of OL gurus from both research and practice domains; its aim is to further highlight the importance of organisational learning so that organisations and individuals know why they should invest in learning. It also helps organizations' management to have a roadmap that can guide them in their learning journey. In spite of the fact that the positioning of the model seem to be influenced by normative language, however, as emphasized throughout the model, it is not meant to be a prescriptive 'cookbook' that may straightjacket organisations and individuals in their endeavor to learn. Rather, we hope the LDO model will help organisations to strategize learning. Strategic learning is about understanding a global strategy and how each business unit in an organisation contributes its best, most innovative thinking followed by actions that execute the strategic intent of the organisation. We believe that strategic learning is the most effective and sustainable approach in helping organisations reaching their strategic objectives; if achieving organisation's strategic objectives is important to organisations, then they need to strategize learning, hence they need to become Learning-Driven Organisations. Although learning could be serendipitous sometimes, however those are one-off cases where organisations cannot rely on co-incidence as they do not know when it will occur. OL has to be structured therefore and embedded into the organisation's ecosystem; in fact it should be an ecosystem in itself. An integrated ecosystem that considers the organisation's culture as 'software' and the organisation typology and dynamics as 'hardware' will definitely lead to accomplishment of strategic intent and realization of the organisation's vision. The next step of the research is to develop the LDO model in the direction of practices because practitioners and executives would prefer having guidelines for practice rather discussing the mere concepts of organisational learning. In our views success and impacts of model such as ISO 9001 and EFQM can be attributed to clarity of the requirements of these models which were informed by research on the one hand and practice on the other hand.

The way forward

The authors have attempted to paint a model that can help organisations, teams and individuals to improve their performance through learning. The LDO model was derived from empirical evidence, literature and practice. However, due to time limitation, the data presented in the empirical evidence was gathered from one sector i.e. hospitality; as such gathering data from other sectors may give further insights and understanding of organisational learning. In addition, it the output of this paper i.e. the proposed LDO model was not tested, therefore, it is planned to undertake further investigation to test the model in various business environment.

References

Akhavan, P., and Jafari, M (2006). 'Learning organizations; the necessity of knowledge era'. Journal of Tadbir, No. 169 (Cited in Saadat and Saadat, 2016)

Antonacopoulou, E. (2006), "Learning-in-practise: the social complexity of learning in working life", AIM working paper series, Advanced Institute of Management Research, London

Argote, L. (2013), Organizational learning: Creating, retaining and transferring knowledge. New York: Springer Science Business Media.

Argote, L. (2011). Organizational Learning Research: Past, Present and Future. Management Learning Journal, Vol. 42, No. 4 pp. 439-446 DOI: 10.1177/1350507611408217

Argyris, C. and Schon, D. (1978) *Organisational Learning: A theory of action perspective*. Cambridge, Mass: Addison Wesley.

Argyris, C. (1996) 'Towards a comprehensive theory of management', in Moingeon, B. and Edmondson, A. (eds) *Organisational Learning and Competitive Advantage*. London: Sage.

Banerjee, P. Gupta, R. and Bates, R. (2017). 'Influence of Organizational Learning Culture on Knowledge Worker's Motivation to Transfer Training: Testing Moderating Effects of Learning Transfer Climate' Current Psychology, Vol. 36, No. 3, pp. 606-617

Bontis, N. Crossan, M.M. and Hulland, J. (2002), "Managing an organizational learning system by aligning stocks and flows", Journal of Management Studies, Vol. 39, No. 4, pp. 437-469

Brockbank, A. McGill, I. and Beech, N. (Edt.) (2002), Reflective Learning in Practice, Gower, England.

Chiva, R., Alegre, J. & Lapiedra, R. (2007), "Measuring organisational learning capability among the workforce", International Journal of Manpower, Vol. 28, No. 3/4, pp. 224-242.

Cirella, S., Ganterino, F, Guerci M., & Shani, A. (2016), Organizational Learning Mechanisms and Creative Climate: Insights from an Italian Fashion Design Company, Journal for Creativity and Innovation Management, Vol. 25 No. 2, pp 211-222.

Cohen, L., Manion, L. and Morrison, K. (2000). *Research Methods in Education* (5th Ed.). London.

Cook, S. and Yanow, D. (1993) 'Culture and Organizational Learning', in M. Cohen and L. Sproull (eds) Organizational Learning, pp. 430–459. Thousand Oaks, CA: Sage Publications.

Crossan, M., Lane, H. and White, R. (1999), "An organizational learning framework: from intuition to institution", Academy of Management Review, Vol. 24 No. 3, pp. 522-37.

DiBella, A. & Nevis, E. (1998) How Organizations Learn: An Integrated Strategy for Building Learning Capability. San Francisco: Jossey-Bass.

Dierkes, M. Antal, A. B. Child, J. and Nonaka, I., (2001). Handbook of Organizational Learning and Knowledge, Oxford University Press.

Dixon N. M. (1999) The Organisational Learning Cycle: How we can learn collectively, 2nd edn. Gower.

Fibuch, E. and Roberston, J. (2017), At Top Organizations Learning Means Living, Physician Leadership Journal, Vol 4, No. 6, pp. 58-62

Fioretti, G. (2007) The Organizational Learning Curve, *European Journal for Operational Research*, Vol. 177, No. 3, pp. 1375-1384.

Friedman, V. J. Lipshitz, R. and Overmeer, W. (2001). Creating Conditions for Organizational Learning (in Dierkes et al Eds, 2001)

Garad, A. (2011). 'The Two Sides of the Same Coin: Organisational Learning and Business Excellence, Case Studies from the Quality Award Winners in the United Arab Emirates' unpublished doctoral thesis. University of Salford, UK.

Garratt, B. (2000) *The Learning Organisation: Developing democracy at work.* London: Harper Collins Business.

Garvin, D.A. (1993), "Building a learning organization", Harvard Business Review, Vol. 71 No. 4, pp. 78-91. (Cited in Islam *et al.* 2015)

Gilaninia, S., Rankouh, M. A., and Gildeh, M. A. (2013) Overview of the Importance of Organisational Learning and Learning Organisation, Journal of Research and Development, Vol. 1, No. 2 pp. 44-49

Guță. A.L. (2014), "Measuring organizational learning. Model testing in two Romanian universities", Management & Marketing. Challenges for the Knowledge Society, Vol. 9, No. 3, pp. 253-282.

Harari, Y., N. (2017), Homo Deus; A Brief History of Tomorrow, Vintage, UK.

Jo, S. & Joo, B. (2011), "Knowledge sharing: the influences of learning organization culture, organizational commitment and organizational citizenship behaviors", Journal of Leadership & Organizational Culture, Vol. 18 No. 3, pp. 353-364.

John, S. (2009). Strategic Learning and Leading Change; How Global Organizations are Reinventing HR', Butterworth-Heinemann, Elsevier Inc.

Jyothibabu, C., Farooq, A. & Pradhan, B.B. (2010), "An integrated scale for measuring an organizational learning system", The Learning Organization, Vol. 17, No. 4, pp. 303-327.

Islam, T., Ahmed, I., & Ahmad, U.N.U, (2015) "The influence of organizational learning culture and perceived organizational support on employees' affective commitment and turnover intention", Nankai Business Review International, Vol. 6 No. 4, pp.417-431, https://doi.org/10.1108/NBRI-01-2015-0002

ISO (2017) ISO 10018:2012, Guidelines on People Involvement and Competence, International Organisation for Standardization, Switzerland

Kolb, D. A. (1984) Experiential Learning: Experience as the source of learning and development. Englewood Cliffs, NJ: Prentice Hall.

Lipshitz, R. Friedman, V., J, and Popper, M., (2007) Demystifying Organizational Learning. California: Sage.

Malik, M.E., Rizwan, Q.D. & Ali, U. (2011), "Impact of motivation to learn and job attitudes on organizational learning culture in a public service organization of Pakistan", African Journal of Business Management, Vol. 5 No. 3, pp. 844-854.

Marsick, V. J., & Watkins, K. E. (2003). Demonstrating the value of an organization's learning culture: The dimensions of the learning organization questionnaire. Advances in Developing Human Resources, Vol. 5 No. 2 pp. 132-151

Marquardt, M.J. (2002), Building The Learning Organization, McGraw Hill, New York, NY.

Mitic, S., Nicolic, M., Jankov, J., Vukonjanski, J., Terek, E. (2017) The impact of information technologies on communication satisfaction and organizational learning in companies in Serbia, Computer in Human Behaviour, Vol. 76, No. pp. 87-101

Mitki, Y., Shani, A.B. & Stjernberg, T. (2008) Leadership Development and Learning

Mechanisms System Transformation as a Balancing Act. Leadership and Organization Development Journal, Vol. 29, pp. 68–84.

Nonaka, I. (1991). 'The knowledge Creating Company'. Harvard Business Review Vol. 69, No. 6. Pp. 96-104

Nonaka, I. and Takeuchi, H. (1995). 'The Knowledge-Creating Company: How Japanese Companies Create the Dynamics of Innovation'. Oxford University Press. New York.

Perryer, C., Jordan, C., Firns, I. & Travaglione, A. (2010), "Predicting turnover intentions: the interactive effects of organizational commitment and perceived organizational support", Management Research Review, Vol. 33 No. 9, pp. 911-923.

Popper, M. and Lipshitz, R. (1998) Organizational Learning Mechanisms: A Cultural and Structural Approach to Organizational Learning. The Journal of Applied Behavioural Science, Vol. 34, pp. 161–79.

Popper, M. and Lipshitz, R. (2000) Organizational Learning: Mechanisms, Culture, and Feasibility. Management Learning, Vol. 31, pp. 181–96.

Popova-Nowak, I.V and Cseh, M. (2015), The Meaning of Organizational Learning; A Meta-paradigm Perspective. Human Resource Development Review, Vol. No. 14 No. 3 pp. 299-331. DOI: 10.1177/1534484315596856

Putz, D., Schilling, J., Kluge, A., and Stangenberg, C. (2012), 'Measuring organizational learning from errors: Development and validation of an integrated model and questionnaire' Management Learning, Vol. 44 No. 5, pp. 511-536

Rebelo, T., M., and Gomes, A., D., (2011) "Conditioning factors of an organizational learning culture", Journal of Workplace Learning, Vol. 23, No. 3, pp.173-194, https://doi.org/10.1108/13665621111117215

Roztocki, N., & Weistroffer, H. R. (2015). Information and communications technology in developing, emerging and transition economies: An assessment of research. Information Technology for Development, Vol 21, No. 3, pp. 330-364.

Saadat, V. and Saadat, Z. (2016). 'Organizational Learning as a Key Role of Organizational Success', Procedia - Social and Behavioural Sciences No. 230 pp. 219 – 225

Schein, E. H. (1990). 'Organizational Culture' American Psychologist, 45: 109-19

Schein, E. H. (2004). 'Organizational Culture and Leadership' Wiley and Son.

Schilling, J. & Kluge, A. (2009). 'Barriers to organizational learning: An integration of theory and research.' International Journal of Management Reviews, Vol. 11, No. 3, pp. 337-360

Shafei, R., Ghaderzadeh, H., Salavati, A. & Lavei, S. (2011), "Survey of relationship between knowledge management and organizational culture dimensions in public organizations: a case of Iranian public organizations", Interdisciplinary Journal of Contemporary Research in Business, Vol. 2 No. 11, pp. 57-70.

Shani, A. B. (R) & Docherty, P. (2003) Learning by Design: Building Sustainable Organizations. Blackwell Publishing, Oxford.

Shani, A. B. (R) & Docherty, P. (2008) Learning by Design: Key Mechanisms in Organization Development. In Cummings, T. (ed.), Handbook of Organizational Change and Development. Sage, Thousand Oaks, CA.

Sharma, R. K. (2003). 'Understanding organizational learning through knowledge management'. Journal of Information and Knowledge Management, Vol. 2 No. 4, pp. 343-352.

Sinek, S. (2009), Start With Why; How Great Leaders Inspire Everyone to Take Action, Penguin Group, USA

Templeton, G. F. Lewis, B. R. and Snyder, C. A. (2002). 'Development of a Measure for Organizational Learning Construct' Journal of Management Information Systems, Vol. 19, No. 2 pp. 175-218

Yang, B., Watkins, K. E., & Marsick, V. J. (2004). The construct of the learning organization: dimensions, measurement, and validation. Human Resource Development Quarterly, 15, 31–55. doi:10.1002/hrdq.1086.

Wahda, (2017) "Mediating effect of knowledge management on organizational learning culture in the context of organizational performance", Journal of Management Development, Vol. 36 No. 7, pp.846-858, https://doi.org/10.1108/JMD-11-2016-0252

Wang, X., Yang, B. & McLean, G. (2007), "Influence of demographic factors and ownership type upon organizational learning culture in Chinese enterprises", International Journal of Training and Development, Vol. 11 No. 3, pp. 154-65.

Weick K.E., and Westley F. (1996), Organizational Learning: Affirming an Oxymoron, In Clegg, S.R, Hardy, C. and Nod, W.R, Handbook of Organisational Studies pp.440-458 London: Sage

Weinzimmer, L. G. and Esken, C. A. (2017). 'Learning From Mistakes: How Mistake Tolerance Positively Affects Organizational Learning and Performance' The Journal of Applied Behavioral Science, Vo. 53 No. 3, pp. 322-348

Wilhelm, W. (2005) 'Learning Architectures: Building Organisational and Individual Learning', 2nd edn. USA: GCA Press

Wittgenstein, L., (1958) Philosophical Investigations, translated by G. E. M. Anscombe, second edition (Oxford: Basil Blackwell)

World Bank (2017) Open Learning Campus Online Portal - Retrieved on 10th July 2017 [URL: https://olc.worldbank.org/content/about-olc]

The Learning-Driven Organisation Model; An Ecosystem for Organisational Learning

Dr. Alaa Garad

Alaa Garad is a highly skilled academic and practitioner with extensive experience in Organisational Learning, and Strategic Quality Management. He has extensive hands-on experience of practical implementations of business tools and techniques across a variety of industries and organisational structures. Published author and a columnist with a proven record of excellence in practice-based teaching, executive training and mentoring. His areas of expertise include ISO Standards, SLAs, Balanced Scorecard, EFQM Excellence Model, Investors in People, action learning, benchmarking, suggestions systems, and mystery shopping. Alaa has designed, delivered and reviewed vast number of syllabuses at both undergraduate and postgraduate levels in addition to supervision of research at master and doctoral levels. Some of his affiliations includes: Fellow, Society for Leadership, St. George House, Fellow, Learning and Performance Institute, Chairman, Egyptian Association for Learning, Executive Board Member at International Foundation for Action Learning, Member, ASQ, BAM, EURAM and AOM.

Professor Jeff Gold

Jeff Gold is Professor of Organisational Learning at York St John University and Leeds Beckett University. He is a strong advocate of the need for actionable knowledge that is rigorously developed but relevant for practice. He has designed and delivered a wide range of seminars, programmes and workshops on talent management and development, change, strategic learning, futures and foresight, management and leadership development with a particular emphasis on participation and distribution. He has worked closely with organisations such as Skipton Building Society, Hallmark Cards, the NHS, the Police Service, Leeds Bradford Boiler Company and a host of others.

www.ingramcontent.com/pod-product-compliance
Lightning Source LLC
Chambersburg PA
CBHW040329220526
45473CB00009B/2626